In a World Created by a Drunken God

In a World Created by a Drunken God

Drew Hayden Taylor

Talonbooks
Vancouver

Talonbooks
P.O. Box 2076, Vancouver, British Columbia, Canada V6B 3S3
www.talonbooks.com

Typeset in Bembo and printed and bound in Canada.

First Printing: 2006

The publisher gratefully acknowledges the financial support of the Canada Council for the Arts; the Government of Canada through the Book Publishing Industry Development Program; and the Province of British Columbia through the British Columbia Arts Council for our publishing activities.

Library and Archives Canada Cataloguing in Publication

Taylor, Drew Hayden, 1962-

    In a world created by a drunken God / Drew Hayden Taylor.

A play.

ISBN 0-88922-537-0

    1. Indians of North America--Drama. 2. Identity (Psychology)--Drama.
I. Title.

PS8589.A885I5 2006   C812'.54   C2005-906205-3

ISBN-10: 0-88922-537-0
ISBN-13: 978-0-88922-537-4

Acknowledgements

In a World Created by a Drunken God was a particularly difficult play for me to write and I could not have done so without a lot of help and support, so I would like to take this opportunity to thank all the people who provided their invaluable assistance in its development and production.

First of all, a big hearty thanks to all the people in my family, especially my mother, who provided me with the strong background and secure upbringing that allowed me to become the kind of individual who makes things up for a living. And I'm not making that up.

Others to whom I owe a debt because they have been instrumental in creating the final stage production of this play include a wonderfully diverse cast of people. Brian Quirt and Factory Theatre's Cross Currents Festival provided me with the first opportunity to actually hear an early draft of this play read, and the National Arts Centre in Ottawa also gave me a chance to see how much further I could take the story than I had originally imagined: thanks Marti and Lise-Ann.

I'm grateful to Tibor Feheregyhazi, Artistic Director of Persephone Theatre in Saskatoon, for having the generosity to finally produce this play after all its developmental work in December, 2004. I would also like to express my gratitude and admiration for the tremendously talented Kennetch Charlette, who directed and starred in that production. Kennetch, I feel, is quickly becoming one of Canada's best interpreters of my work.

Thanks also to Trish Warner, who provided the medical information—now there's someone who knows her kidneys.

And a special thanks to the lovely Janine, who provided me with the emotional support I needed while writing this play.

—Drew Hayden Taylor

In a World Created by a Drunken God was publicly workshopped at Factory Theatre in Toronto as part of the 2003 Cross Currents Festival. It premiered at Persephone Theatre in Saskatoon on December 2, 2004 with the following cast and crew:

HARRY DEITER . . . . Kent Allen
JASON PIERCE . . . . . Kennetch Charlette

Director . . . . Kennetch Charlette
Set designer . . . . Hans Becker
Costumes designer . . . . . Theresa Germain
Lighting designer . . . . Mark von Eschen
Stage manager . . . . Laura Kennedy
Fight director . . . . Kent Allen

Characters

HARRY DEITER, *a 31-year-old American non-Native man.*

JASON PIERCE, *a 31-year-old Canadian half-Native man.*

Setting

This play takes place in a small apartment in downtown Toronto. The time is a contemporary September late afternoon.

ACT ONE

*Lights up on a one-bedroom apartment. There
are boxes piled everywhere and material
scattered about, in the process of being packed.
Half-empty shelves and barren walls are
evident. JASON PIERCE, a man of mixed
Native/non-Native ancestry, enters the room
with an armload of clothes, which he starts
stuffing neatly into garbage bags. At one point,
realizing he is hungry, he stops, picks up the
phone and starts dialling. He's halfway through
the number when he realizes the phone is dead.*

JASON
 Shit ... forgot.

*He approaches the refrigerator and peers into it.
It is empty. Dejected, he opens a packing box
and rummages through it until he finds a box
of Kraft Dinner. He opens it and pours out
some of the uncooked, hard noodles into his
hand and eats them. Crunching away happily,
he returns to immaculately packing clothes into
the bags. He is humming a song to himself.
When he is done, he returns to his bedroom.
While out of the room, the doorbell rings. And*

*rings again. Arms full of clothes, JASON runs
back into the room, dumping them on the couch
as he answers the door.*

*Standing outside JASON's apartment is
HARRY DEITER, a well-dressed non-Native
man. He looks nervous and ill at ease.*

JASON

Oh, hi … I guess you must be the new tenant.
You're a little early. I was told I had the rest of the
day. The moving truck won't be here for another
two hours, so I'm sorry but you'll have to …

HARRY

No. I'm not the new tenant. Are you Jason Pierce?

JASON

Yeah. Who are you?

HARRY

Harry. Harry Deiter.

JASON

Well, hello Harry. Harry Deiter.

There is an awkward pause.

So if you're not the new guy who's gonna live
here, who the hell are you and what can I do for

you? I'm in a little bit of a hurry. I should have
finished this last night but … well, you know.

HARRY

    May I come in?

JASON

    Not until you explain why you know me and why
    you're here.

HARRY

    It's kind of awkward. Please?

    Pressed for time, JASON lets him enter.

JASON

    Suit yourself.

    *HARRY enters, looking around. He is even
    more nervous. JASON goes back to packing.*

    Mind if I do this while you talk? Would you like
    some Kraft noodles? It's all I've got for munchies.

HARRY

    No, thank you. Go ahead, don't let me interrupt.
    My name is …

JASON

    Harry. Harry Deiter. You already told me.

HARRY

Yes. Sorry. And you're Jason Pierce.

JASON

I think we've already gone through that. Now why do you know me when I don't know you?

HARRY

That ... is a story. This is your apartment. I see you're moving.

JASON

Yeah, another couple of hours and you would have missed me completely. I'm moving back home.

HARRY

To Otter Lake.

JASON stops packing.

JASON

Okay, you're starting to scare me. Who the fuck are you and why do you know where I'm from?

HARRY

That's a very good question. This is kind of awkward.

There is an awkward pause.

Umm ...

JASON

Umm … ?

HARRY

Mr. Pierce. Look at me. Do I look at all familiar to you?

JASON

Never seen you before in my life. Don't change the subject. Who the hell are you?

HARRY

I'm not changing the subject. Take a close look at my face. Are you sure there's nothing there remotely familiar?

JASON

Sorry, I don't look closely into a lot of men's faces. You've got kind of a funny accent. Not a Canadian one, American I'd say.

HARRY

Very astute of you. I'm from Providence, Rhode Island.

JASON

Never been there. Cut the games and tell me why you were knocking at my door, knowing way more about me than most Americans should. You with one of those FBI, CIA, three-lettered organizations?

Did I do something wrong when I was in
Michigan last year?

HARRY

I'm not exactly sure how much you know or have
been told but does Providence or Rhode Island
mean anything to you?

JASON

There's a huge Indian casino about an hour away.
Look, I gotta pack ...

*JASON tries to lead HARRY out the door but
HARRY resists.*

HARRY

No, please. I'm not handling this right. You have to
forgive me, this is all so new to me, too. I have to
talk to you about something. It's very important. In
fact, it's a matter of life and death.

JASON

WHAT IS?! Either tell me what this is all about or
get out. I'm in too much of a hurry to play games.

HARRY

Okay. Okay. I am your brother ... half-brother
actually.

JASON

My half-brother … I don't have any brothers. Sisters either. I'm an only child. The FBI's been feeding you some wrong information, my friend. Complain to your congressman. You can let yourself out now. I think you remember where the door is.

HARRY

Your mother's name is Harriet Pierce. She'd be almost sixty now. Your reservation is about three hours due north of here. And your father was not an Indian. He was an American.

Pause.

JASON

First of all, Harry, Harry Deiter, it's called a *reserve* up here in Canada. And we're called First Nations, not Indians …

HARRY

That's all you have to say?

JASON

That and you've got to be lying.

HARRY

I'm not.

JASON stares at HARRY long and hard.

JASON

You can't be.

HARRY

I am.

JASON

A lot of people could say what you're saying. I
don't suppose you can prove it.

HARRY

Not directly. I just have the word of my ... our
father. And I can see him in your chin. There is a
certain facial and bodily similarity between us.
Haven't you ever wondered about this?

JASON

Sorry, any white American can show up claiming
anything. Your CIA is famous for that. I don't
believe you. I don't need this. You picked a bad
time for practical jokes 'cause I don't find this very
funny. Now get out before I throw you out.

HARRY

I'm here ...

JASON

> I don't care why you're here. You are not here. Go away. It's still my apartment and I've got a lot of things to do. The door ...

HARRY

> His name is ...

JASON

> I don't care.

HARRY

> ... Lawrence Deiter.

JASON

> I DON'T CARE!

HARRY

> This is important. I assure you.

JASON

> What is it with you Americans? You can never take a hint. If this was important, all this would have happened thirty years ago, and we wouldn't be having this conversation.

HARRY

> Then you believe me.

JASON

> If it will end this conversation sooner, yes I believe
> you. Sure, whatever. It doesn't change anything. If
> you are my half-brother, and this Lawrence Deiter
> is my father ... in the big scheme of existence, my
> life hasn't changed much since ten minutes ago.
> Everything is still the same. Luckily it's not much
> of an issue for me. But thank you for the
> information, I will treasure it always but I've got a
> sock drawer to empty. Goodbye. Again.

HARRY

> He's dying.

> *JASON stops in his tracks.*

JASON

> It just gets better and better, doesn't it?

HARRY

> Our father. He's dying.

JASON

> That's why you're here. I'd send him a card but I
> don't know where he lives, what he does or if he
> knows who I am.

HARRY

> Oh he knows who you are. He's the one that told
> me. He told me to come and find you.

JASON

He's a little late in that department, isn't he?

HARRY

He was afraid you might be a little bitter.

JASON

Ya think?!

HARRY

He says he only saw you once. When you were two months old.

JASON

That sounds about right.

HARRY

He regrets the way things happened.

No comment from JASON.

JASON

Why are you here?

HARRY

I told you. He's dying.

JASON

And what's that got to do with me?

*HARRY wanders around the room, trying to
gather up the strength to talk.*

HARRY

I had an apartment like this, years ago, before I got
married. You married?

JASON

No.

HARRY

Technically neither am I. Divorced, but I've got
two great kids out of it. Colin and Angela. They're
four and six. Do you have any kids?

JASON

Not that I know of.

*HARRY stops in front of a large poster, a
parody of the Canadian flag, but in green.*

HARRY

That's the Canadian flag, isn't it?

JASON

That's a cannabis leaf, not a maple leaf. And it's
supposed to be red, not green.

*A slightly embarrassed HARRY opens one
cardboard box and brings out some books.*

HARRY

I don't travel much outside the States. Ah, you're a reader. You can tell a lot about a man by what he reads.

JASON

They're mostly Native books.

HARRY

Portraits of the Whiteman, Custer Died for Your Sins, Where Whitemen Fear to Tread. Hmm, I'm sensing a trend here ... Do you ever read anything less hostile?

JASON

Sometimes. So he's dying. What do you want me to do about it?

HARRY

Well ... funny you should ask that. I'm a fund-raiser. A professional fund-raiser. I work for a hospital in Rhode Island. Last year I managed a campaign that raised over $6 million for the hospital. I'm very good at what I do. Our campaign slogan was "There are three types of people in the world. Those that poison wells. Those that mow the lawn. And those that build hospitals. Which one are you?" I came up with that original concept. It's based on a saying my father has. The hospital board wanted to hire an advertising firm and give them

ten grand for something similar but in the end, my
slogan seemed the most appropriate. My point here
being, Jason, of these three types of people, which
one are you?

JASON

I grew up mowing the lawn. Made a small fortune
as a kid from mowing the lawn. Grass will never
stop growing and ice skates weren't on my poor
single mother's budget. Guess what I'm doing
tomorrow at my mother's house once I unpack?

HARRY

You're missing the point, Jason. These three types of
people ...

JASON

Are you pitching me something? Does my place
look like it can afford to donate money to a
hospital in Rhode Island? And I don't believe I
gave you the right to call me by my first name.

HARRY

Please ... perhaps I should start at the beginning.

JASON

Or not at all. I doubt this will interest me. I've got
a life of my own, one that needs my complete
concentration. And I got past caring about the
interests of Larry Deiter long ago.

HARRY

Lawrence. He hates being called Larry. Our
father ...

JASON walks out of the room. HARRY
attempts to follow him but is hit by a shower of
clothes at the doorway.

JASON

No.

HARRY

Mr. Pierce ...

JASON

No.

HARRY

Please ...

JASON

NO!

HARRY unconsciously puts the t-shirts neatly
down on the couch, until he notices what's on
the t-shirts.

HARRY

Do all your t-shirts have First Nations slogans on
them? My god, there must be a couple of dozen.

> *JASON enters the living room carrying even more t-shirts with slogans.*

JASON

I work at a lot of conferences.

HARRY

He needs a kidney.

> *JASON doesn't respond.*

For a transplant. That's why I'm here.

JASON

From me? He needs a kidney ... from me. Oh my god ... this ... this is a bad movie. I don't believe this. Where's your bucket or are you going to carry my kidney in your pocket?

> *JASON exits again.*

HARRY

No, no ... take it easy. I just want you to take a little test. I admit this is a little unorthodox. Trust me, I wouldn't be bothering you if this wasn't an emergency. We only found out eight months ago that his kidneys were failing. Something called chronic renal failure. His kidneys were just deteriorating, shutting down. And there's nothing the doctors can do. For the last two months he's

been on dialysis, and he needs a transplant if he's
going to live. He needs one soon.

There is no response from the bedroom.

I know this is kind of a shock. I show up at your
door and lay this all on you, but he's going to die.
Because of some weird genetic shit, none of our
family is compatible. That's when the doctor asked
him if there were any other family members that
could be tested. At first Dad didn't want to say
anything, but …

JASON storms into the room.

JASON

Did he tell you about the last time he saw me or
my mother? What did he say to you? About us?

HARRY

You have to understand. He's very sick. It's difficult
for him to talk very much. All this has put such a
strain on him. On all of us.

JASON

What did he tell you?

HARRY

Just that he met your mother when he was hunting
up here in Ontario. Near your reservation …
reserve …

JASON

Is that all?

HARRY

I didn't really ask. This was a bit of a shock to me too, you know. My father admitting to an affair … Fathers are supposed to be perfect, you know? The important thing is you might have the ability to save him. But I'm the only one who knows about you. My mother thinks I'm off on some business trip and …

JASON

So your mother doesn't know, huh? Yeah, why should she, huh? Another son somewhere up in Canada is really none of her business. How considerate of him. So how old are you?

HARRY

Thirty-four. What has that got to do with anything?

JASON

Hmm, you were three years old when I was born. Did he tell you that?

HARRY

I know you probably have some issues with him … and rightly so, but try to see the bigger picture.

He's dying. And you have the capacity to build that hospital.

JASON

The gentleman of whom you speak left right after I was born. To go back to his existing family in the States, I was told. That's all I ever knew about him. I guess hunting season was over and he went back to you and your mother. People often ask if I ever missed having a father, but how can you miss something you never had? It's like asking somebody who's always been blind if they miss being able to see. It's different yet the same. Luckily I'm not bitter.

HARRY

I can tell.

JASON

And now he wants a kidney. Now that would be a hell of a Father's Day present, huh?

HARRY

All we want is to see if you're compatible. It's a simple blood test. That's not much to ask.

JASON

And what if I am compatible?

HARRY

We can discuss that when the time comes.

JASON

The thing is, I'm kinda partial to my bodily organs, and I don't just go around sharing them with strangers. I don't know anything about him. Or about you. Or about the wonderful state of Rhode Island. I'm just a poor Canadian Indian.

HARRY

I thought you said you were called First Nations up here?

JASON

First thing to know about Canadian First Nations people is we hate being corrected. What I call myself is none of your business. My point is, I don't know you and this is a big decision to make on such little information. Tell me about yourself.

HARRY

I'm not really the issue here.

JASON

No, my kidneys are. So, fill me in on the Deiter family. You've got two kids, an ex-wife and a loving mother and father. The American dream. Did you grow up in Providence?

HARRY

Yes.

JASON

Do Mom and Pop live there too?

HARRY

No, they live just outside the city, in a town called
Cranston.

JASON

What does he do for a living?

HARRY

He owns and operates a successful hotel.

JASON

And you. You're divorced. When? How?

HARRY

That doesn't concern you.

JASON

I'm just curious. You seem to have hit a rather
severe hiccup on the road of love. I myself am in
the process of leaving an unfortunate relationship
behind and literally packing up and moving on.
Sound familiar? Coincidence ... or heredity, you
think? Mom and Dad are still married?

HARRY

Of course.

JASON

But your mom doesn't know about my mom.
Or me. Or the process by which I ended up on
Mother Earth all those decades ago?

HARRY

My father explained that it was a long time ago. He
was a different man back then. He regrets it. It
would destroy her if he told her now. She's already
upset over his illness. She doesn't need to know.

JASON

So he regrets it, huh?

HARRY

He didn't mean it that way.

JASON

Of course not. When did you get divorced?

HARRY

Two years ago, if it's really that important to you.

JASON

How long were you married?

HARRY

Seven years. You?

JASON

We weren't married. Just sharing this apartment of passion for five years, till she told me she loved me but wasn't in love with me. A subtle but distinctive difference, I'm told. Yours?

HARRY

She was a bitch.

JASON

Is that you or the alimony talking?

HARRY

Many things were involved in our marriage ending. Neither of us cheated on the other, or was abusive. It just ended through a mutual and growing lack of respect. I developed an overactive work ethic and she developed an unwelcome and highly utilized temper, which I didn't think was healthy for the children to witness. As a result, she devised a series of pet names for me. "Stupid," "useless," "wuss" and "a baby" were some of the more colourful ones, but my favourite was "toxic." Evidently I was toxic, whatever that means. So she told me to change. I did. I became single. Enough?

JASON

> Sounds like it was a bad divorce.

HARRY

> You could say that. And then there were her ...
> hobbies. I swear, that woman just about feng-shuied
> me to death.

JASON

> What the hell is that?

HARRY

> Some sort of Chinese river of energy thing. Since
> we were having difficulties, she thought that maybe
> rearranging the furniture would help somehow.
> Smooth things out. After putting the couch and
> dining room table in half a dozen places, she finally
> gave up and we divorced. Somehow I just think
> Dutch women weren't meant to practice feng shui.
> Why did ... what's your ex's name?

JASON

> Bonnie.

HARRY

> Mine's was Arlene. What happened with Bonnie?

JASON

> Hey! I'm asking the questions here.

HARRY

I was merely curious.

Pause.

JASON

Tell me if you understand this. She tells me that before me, she used to go out with this guy out west. They were both park rangers and they spent about two years together. The problem was that the guy was married ... actually separated, and wanted to get back with his wife. So not wanting to come between him and his wife and kids, she backed away and moved back here to Ontario. That's where I entered the picture. She always described him as the love of her life. But hey, everybody has a past so I had no problem with that. I've got a few stories in my own background, so I say *c'est la vie* ... That's French, we have two official languages in Canada and that means ...

HARRY

I'm familiar with the term

JASON

So a couple of months ago she got word that he was divorced and moving to Ottawa to work for the government. She said she needed to either find out if what she felt was still there or find "closure."

So basically I got dumped for a memory. For a guy she hadn't seen in seven years.

HARRY

That must have hurt.

JASON

This guy could be a hundred pounds overweight, bald, no teeth and missing a leg. I mean I thought we had a good thing going … evidently not. So I thought, fuck her. Fuck this city. Fuck everything. I'm going home because you can't compete with a memory. So does any of that make sense? The whole bird-in-the-hand thing …

HARRY

You're asking the wrong guy. Do you want to know what the true irony of my failed marriage is? Have you ever heard of the International Star Registry?

JASON

Is that some sort of Hollywood union thing?

HARRY

No. It's an organization that names stars. The ones up in the sky. Actually it's a brilliant marketing concept. There are so many stars in this galaxy that most of them are given just numbers. So, from

Earth, we can see about 100 billion, give or take a few. So this company, for a fee, will let you name a star. You get a certificate and a star map and everything. Ten years ago it cost me something like thirty dollars to name a star after Arlene. At the time it was terribly romantic. Somewhere out there, on the other side of Orion's belt, is the Star Arlene, and it will be giving off light and warmth billions of years after our marriage has gone cold and after we both have died. In a thousand years my great-great-great-great-grandchildren will be surveying the Arlene solar system unless the whole thing blows up in a supernova. Have you ever heard of anything more stupid?

> *JASON pauses for a moment, debating, then rolls up his t-shirt sleeve to reveal a large elaborate tattoo, with the name Bonnie at the centre.*

JASON

The stupid things you do when you're twenty-seven. Man, that's going to be a bitch to get off. Number one on my things-to-do list once I'm settled. You name a star and I get a tattoo … Maybe we *are* brothers, huh?

HARRY

Anything else you want to know about us?

JASON

So he's dying, huh? And you thought because of
simple biology, I'd simply wanna help? Here, what's
a kidney amongst family, that kind of thing?

HARRY

You wouldn't be here without him.

JASON

Exactly. Without him, I wouldn't be here. How'd
you find me, anyways?

HARRY

It wasn't that hard. I did a little research. My father
remembered your name. I phoned Otter Lake, the
city hall ...

JASON

The band office ...

HARRY

Of course, the band office. They told me you lived
in Toronto. Directory assistance. I booked a flight
immediately. That was five days ago. And now I'm
here.

JASON

And now you're here. My half-brother from
America. How about that?

HARRY

> I also did some additional research. There's a hospital near here that does the kind of tests I've been mentioning. I've taken the liberty of setting up an appointment at Toronto General Hospital. I don't suppose you know what blood type you are?

JASON

> Sorry. No blood tests.

HARRY

> You have to.

JASON

> You've taken our language, our land, our culture, but I'm not letting you have my kidney. An Indian has to draw the line somewhere. Let me ask you: would you, Harry, Harry Deiter, go through all of this yourself for a complete stranger?

HARRY

> He's not a complete stranger. He's your father!

JASON.

> That's merely a noun. I've never met the noun. He took one look at me at the ripe age of two months and left the country, again. I believe that negates any responsibility I might have towards him. I saw it on *Law & Order*. Give him your own kidney.

HARRY

I told you, mine doesn't match.

JASON

Maybe mine doesn't either. Maybe I got one of those weird genetic mismatches you were talking about earlier. You know, because they're contaminated by Aboriginal chromosomes.

HARRY

You don't know that.

JASON

This chronic renal thing …

HARRY

Chronic renal failure.

JASON

It's not a hereditary thing, is it?

HARRY

No. You're our last chance.

JASON

For him to tell you about me and his past indiscretions, it would have to be serious, wouldn't it? How did he tell you? About me, I mean.

HARRY

Is this really necessary?

JASON

Again, my kidney.

HARRY

First of all. He's a wonderful man.

JASON

I'll take your word for it. My mother's a wonderful
woman, too. How about that, they're both
wonderful people. It's a small world. (*Pause.*) Well,
you gonna tell me or should I continue packing
my things?

HARRY

Last week, in his hospital room. We were alone. My
aunt and uncle had taken my mother to the cafeteria
for something to eat. It was all we could do to get
her out of my father's room, especially after she had
learned nobody in the family was compatible. But
evidently that was what he was waiting for. He
called me over to his bed and told me.

JASON

Ah, confession is good for the soul. You guys must
be Catholic. What exactly did he tell you? I'm all
ears.

HARRY

He told me that a long time ago, he and his friends
would go up to Canada to go hunting every year.

JASON

And did he tell you how he bagged more than just deer?

HARRY

Don't be vulgar. My father's not like that.

JASON

You know him better than I do. But you were saying …

HARRY

He was telling me about coming up here to go hunting. And they'd employ local Indian … First Nations people as guides. And while he was there, he met a woman …

JASON

Yes, I'm listening.

HARRY

He … developed a relationship with her one summer and when he and his friends returned the following year …

JASON

There I was. And he left again.

HARRY

He never meant to hurt anybody. You must realize
that. It's just that he had other obligations … a
family in Providence.

JASON

I guess a knocked-up Native woman didn't fit into
the big picture, did it?

HARRY

I'm not condoning what he did but times were
different back then. He panicked.

JASON

Oh? Would you have handled the situation
differently?

HARRY

I can't answer that.

JASON

That's funny. I can. But maybe my background
gives me a special insight. What was your reaction
when he told you about me?

HARRY

How do you think I reacted?! I was stunned, hurt
… this was my father confessing to me that he had

cheated on my mother ... that he had another
child besides me ... I ... I didn't know what to say.
But I realized now wasn't the time to be upset. I
could deal with my disappointment in him later,
when he's healthy again. He suggested I try and
find you.

JASON

Not for me, but for my kidney. It's almost a
heartwarming story. Or a kidney-warming story.

HARRY

Sarcasm isn't helping the situation.

JASON

Sarcasm's all I've got right now. That and a kidney.

*Suddenly HARRY's phone goes off. He answers
it.*

HARRY

Hello ... (*Pause.*) oh, hi Mom. (*Pause.*) No, I'm
with ... the specialist right now. Can I call you
back? (*Pause.*) I'll get home as soon as I can. I
promise. Give Dad a hug for me. I'll call later.
(*Pause.*) Yes, I know. Bye.

HARRY hangs up.

JASON

Where does she think you are?

HARRY

New York.

JASON

My phone's been disconnected. Mind if I borrow
yours for a second? I'll be quick, I promise.

HARRY hands over his phone.

Cool phone. (*dials*) Hey Mom, how's things?
(*Pause.*) No, just wanted to let you know I'm
almost all packed. Depending on traffic, I should be
getting there by nine-ish. I just wanted to remind
you to leave the garage door open so I can unload
everything as quickly as possible. These guys get
paid by the hour, you know. (*Pause.*) Oh, you know
my life, Mom, never a dull moment. I'm here with
a friend of mine, Harry, he's helping me pack.
(*Pause.*) Oh yeah, he's like a brother to me.
Anyways, gotta go wrap things up. Take care, Mom.
I love you. Bye.

*JASON hangs up the phone and hands it back
to HARRY.*

That was my mom. I'm moving back in with her
until I can find work and a place of my own. To

the best of my knowledge, she doesn't have any
skeletons or unknown children in her closet. That's
the great thing about my mother, no great
surprises.

HARRY

She sounds like a very nice woman.

JASON

I think so. Ask Lawrence. He thought so too, way
back when. If you want, I'll introduce you to her
someday.

HARRY

That won't be necessary.

JASON

Now you see, that's a big difference between
Native people and non-Native people. I've
extended a courtesy to you. Of meeting my
mother. Somehow I don't expect you to return the
invitation.

HARRY

You know that's not possible.

JASON

For my kidney, I don't suppose I could get thirty
years of back child support?

HARRY

> This isn't funny. I realize this is an awkward
> situation but my father is dying in a hospital and
> there's nothing I can do to stop it. Except come
> here and convince you to put aside any difficulties
> you might have. He's a frail, sixty-year-old man.
> Here, I have a picture ...

> > *HARRY pulls his wallet out and tries to show a*
> > *photograph to JASON, but JASON doesn't*
> > *want to see it.*

> See, that's him with my kids, his grandchildren.
> He's ...

JASON

> Take that away from me. I don't want to see him. I
> got over wanting that a long time ago. He's your
> father, not mine.

HARRY

> Just look ...

> > *JASON grabs the wallet and throws it across the*
> > *apartment. HARRY retrieves it.*

JASON

> I don't care what he looks like. I don't care how
> healthy he is. I don't care what he told his wife.
> And I don't care how much he means to you. I've

gone thirty-one years without a father and it's a
little late now for me to need one. If I look at that
picture, it would mean I was curious. And I'm not.
I think I've wasted enough time on this issue. I
hope you've enjoyed your visit to Canada, be sure
to pick up some Tim Hortons coffee on your way
to the airport. It's one of the things we Canadians
are famous for, because Kidneys-R-Us is about to
close. You'd better hurry up, there's a curfew on
Americans in this town.

HARRY

No.

JASON

I'm sorry?

HARRY

I'm not leaving. I refuse to. This is too important an
issue to let you throw me out on a whim. You're
letting the wounded little boy deep inside you
make life-threatening decisions.

JASON

Don't make me throw you out. In the mood I'm
in, I might enjoy it too much.

HARRY

Go ahead. If I leave this apartment by myself, my
father's dead. There is nothing you could possibly

do to me that would be worse than that. Even you
should be able to figure that out. So do your worst.

> *HARRY plops himself down in a chair and puts
> his feet up. There is an ominous silence. JASON
> assesses his options.*

JASON
Fine. Amuse yourself.

> *JASON goes back to stuffing clothes in the
> garbage bags. He also packs a few remaining
> things in boxes, trying hard to ignore HARRY.
> HARRY watches him closely. JASON begins to
> hum a song to himself.*

HARRY
What's that song you're humming?

JASON
"Crazy" by Patsy Cline.

HARRY
You're a country music fan

JASON
Bonnie was.

> *More silence except for JASON's humming and
> packing. JASON suddenly grabs HARRY's*

*phone and dials a number. He waits a second
then starts singing into the phone.*

JASON

"Crazy. I'm crazy for feeling so lonely.
I'm crazy."

He then hangs up and goes back to packing.

HARRY

What was all that about?

JASON

What?

HARRY

The phone call, the song?

JASON

I just called Bonnie's answering machine. She's one
of those people who when they hear a song with a
memorable melody, it gets stuck in her head and
bounces around in there for a few days. Drives her
nuts. I do this every once in a while for the hell of
it. That "ooga chaka, ooga ooga" song just about
sent her to the hospital.

HARRY

That's very cruel. I must remember that.

JASON goes back to work.

I'm more into blues myself.

JASON doesn't reply.

Do you listen to any blues?

JASON

> No, I don't listen to any blues. Is this what you're
> gonna do, just sit here and ask me pointless
> questions?

HARRY

> Yep.

JASON

> Well, here's a question for you. Has it possibly
> occurred to you that people are creatures of habit?
> That when we do something, chances are we will
> probably do it again and again? Simple psychology.

HARRY

> So?

JASON

> Maybe your father is a creature of habit. Maybe my
> mother wasn't the only Indian in the cupboard, if
> you know what I mean. Maybe there are other
> brothers and sisters out there, dozens of them, with
> even more dozens of kidneys fresh for the picking,
> and you're sitting here wasting time talking about

the blues when I'm sure one of them would be more than delighted to be sliced open for dear old Dad. Did you ever think of that?

HARRY

My father's not like that.

JASON

Have you forgotten whose chair you're sitting in? But have you even considered it? For a second. Contrary to popular belief, lightning does strike twice.

HARRY

There was nobody else.

JASON

You sound so sure.

HARRY

I am.

JASON

Maybe naive is a better word.

HARRY

I am not naive. You should have seen him when he told me. It was like a huge weight had been lifted from his chest. In a way, he was glad he told me.

Relieved, in fact. He'd been carrying it for so long.
The guilt from … that … taught him a lesson.
There's just me and you.

JASON

You're way too trusting. Maybe it's all that
American "mom's apple pie" stuff I hear about. He
just told you and your family one little thing. Only
because it just might save his life. There could be a
whole lot of other things he's conveniently
forgetting to mention. A selective memory can be
habit-forming.

HARRY

Drop it. Now.

JASON

Touched a nerve, have I? So tell me, Harry, Harry
Deiter, when you were married, did you ever …
see another star you wanted to name?

HARRY

No. I said we didn't cheat on each other.

JASON

Like father, not like son?

HARRY

Did you? On Bonnie?

JASON

I'm talking about you.

HARRY

But I'm talking about you. You're trying to change the subject. Maybe there's more to Bonnie's leaving than what you told me.

JASON

Hey, I'm the first to admit it. I'm not perfect. I was at a hockey tournament a few years ago. I bumped into an old girlfriend. I'm not proud of it, but hey, these things happen.

HARRY

So let me get this straight, you can do whatever you want behind your girlfriend's back, but you can criticize my father all you want for essentially the same thing?

JASON

But here's the difference. Bonnie and I weren't married. We'd only been going out for a year. We didn't have any children. And if anything had happened from that, like a kid, I'd like to think I might not have been so quick to run off to another country, conveniently forgetting the issue. Call me old-fashioned with a conscience but ...

HARRY

That's just different icing on the same cake. Let he who is without sin …

JASON

… send their son to clean up their messes? Tell you what, if he wants my kidney so badly, let him come and get it himself. I'm sure he knows where my mother lives. I'll keep it warm till then. Think he'll be interested?

HARRY

Are you insane? He's in a fucking hospital. He can't get out of the goddamned bed, let alone fly up here.

JASON

If he wants to really cleanse his conscience, and get his hands on my kidney so badly, here I am. He should know to never send a boy to do a man's work.

HARRY

You can't be this shallow and uncaring.

JASON

Sure I can. You don't know me. You don't know me at all. And neither does your father. So you're in no position to pass judgement. But I am. My predicament practically demands it. You don't like it, you know where the door is.

There is a silence.

When I was seven, I asked my mother why, on Father's Day, everybody made a Father's Day card at school. She told me to make one for my grandfather instead. "He's everything you need for a father," she said. And she was right. I never really understood those nuclear family type shows like *Leave It to Beaver.* I suppose you had the *Cosby Show / Seventh Heaven* type of upbringing? Picnics, baseball games, being taught how to ride a bike?

HARRY doesn't answer.

No answer?

HARRY

Those are just television shows. No real family is like that.

JASON

Or was your family more the *Married with Children / The Sopranos* type deal?

HARRY

Now you're being ridiculous. We were a normal family.

JASON

I've actually never met a normal family. (*Pause.*) You look nervous.

HARRY

We're wasting time.

JASON

I'm not. I'm busy. I'm packing. I'm going on with my life. Like I've always done. In fact, if you'll excuse me, I must go put these kidneys to good use. Amuse yourself.

JASON exits to the bathroom. Suffering from nervous energy, HARRY wanders the room. He finds an open box and something catches his eye. He pulls out a framed picture and looks at it. Suddenly, the bathroom door opens, the sound of flushing in the background. HARRY quickly tries to put the picture back in the box but it falls to the ground. It breaks. He quickly picks up all the pieces.

HARRY

I'm sorry. I'm sorry.

JASON

Why did you break my mother's picture?

HARRY

It was an accident. I saw it lying there in the box and I got curious. I ... I ... didn't mean ...

JASON takes the picture from HARRY.

JASON

That's me and her at her birthday party. Fifty-eight years old.

HARRY

I'll replace the frame.

JASON

Forget the frame. What do you think of my mother?

HARRY

Um ... It's a good picture. Um ... She looks very ... uh ... Indi ... First Nations.

JASON

Her first language is Ojibway.

HARRY

Good for her. Arlene was pretty good at Dutch. The kids haven't picked it up though. (*Pause.*) To tell you the truth, I've never really met a lot of First Nations people. There's not too many of them in Rhode Island. At least not that you'd recognize.

Went to Foxwoods a couple of times, you know,
the Pequot casino, but it's hard to tell who's who
there. I think all you guys were killed off a couple
of hundred years ago. Sorry.

JASON

"You guys"? Not my guys, Ojibways don't eat a
lot of lobster. You'll find more Ojibways in Florida
than Rhode Island.

HARRY

Florida? Why?

JASON

The beaches are better.

HARRY

A few years back I was going to take my family to
that big festival ... what do they call it ... a pow
wow ... the one they hold just outside of Hartford,
Connecticut. Schim ... Schim ...

JASON

Schimitzen.

HARRY

That's the place. But Arlene came down with the
flu that weekend and we never made it. That
happens when you have kids. So you grew up on
one of these reserves?

JASON

> Till I moved to Ottawa for work, then Sudbury,
> London and a few other places. Now I'm going full
> circle. Home sweet home.

HARRY

> What exactly do you do for a living?

JASON

> I cook. I'm a cook with aspirations to chefdom.
> The knowledge of cooking is one of the benefits
> you get from being the product of a single mom
> who was working all the time. I was frying my
> own eggs when I was ten.

HARRY

> I'm a Lean Cuisine kind of guy.

JASON

> You should have been here last week. I threw
> myself my own little going-away party and I made
> a venison roast that would make you cry. Venison's
> very lean. And it qualifies as cuisine. That's one of
> the reasons my mother's so glad I'm moving home.
> She misses my cooking. Now there's a switch, huh?

HARRY

> Did your mother ever speak about my father?
> Anything?

JASON

Once, when I was about sixteen. She said she felt
she owed it to me.

HARRY

What did she say?

JASON

That is between her and me. And not you.

HARRY

I'd really like to know.

JASON

Just tell your father ... she's not bitter. As she says,
these things happen.

HARRY

Maybe you could learn something from her.

JASON

Oh, I have. Lots of things. My mother has the most
amazing memory. It comes from being part of an
oral culture. She remembers everything. And so do
I. It's just that she's a much more forgiving person
than I am. She'd give you a kidney. Whereas I will
not. Like mother, not like son.

HARRY

Maybe if I phoned her and explained the
situation ...

JASON

I would beat the living crap out of you. You can't
get my kidney so you want hers ...

HARRY

No no, she wouldn't be compatible. But she might
be able to talk some sense into you.

JASON

No.

HARRY

I'm desperate.

JASON

So am I. You don't know how to get a hold of her.

HARRY

I could drive there. Ask around. I'm sure she
wouldn't be that difficult to find. Or better yet,
you just called your mother on my phone. I'll just
check call history.

*JASON grabs the phone and tosses it across the
room, where it lands on a pile of boxes.*

JASON

I won't let you.

HARRY

I'm past desperate now.

*HARRY rushes past JASON, looking for the
phone, but JASON grabs him.*

JASON

I said no.

*JASON throws HARRY with all his might
towards the door. A bit of a tussle occurs with
neither getting the upper hand.*

Get out of my apartment!

Finally JASON gets on top of HARRY.

You've been sitting behind a desk too long. At least
I still play some hockey.

*HARRY manages to dislodge JASON from on
top of him, and the tables are reversed.*

HARRY

I play racquetball.

They pause in position, out of breath.

JASON

So what now, Harry, Harry Deiter? Gonna drag me
to the hospital by the scruff of my neck?

HARRY gets up and lets JASON get up.
HARRY looks defeated.

HARRY

I don't know. I can't make you do this. I don't
know how. I'm ... I'm at an end. I guess you are a
well poisoner.

JASON

Go home, Harry. Go home to your father and
mother. There's nothing for you here, except me.
And the only place I'm going is to my home. The
truth be told, I don't have any animosity towards
you. And as for your father ... I'd have to think of
him to have an opinion. And I prefer not to. I just
don't like the idea that simply because of a
biological relationship, you have expectations of
me. That's presumptuous. Incredibly presumptuous.
I agree that family is very important, but there's a
hell of a lot more to family than a few strands of
DNA. What if the tables were turned, and I needed
a kidney, or a bone marrow transplant, or
something like that? Would he offer himself up for
me? I'm sure he would for you, but what about

me? How far does this biological obligation
extend? Does it work both ways?

HARRY doesn't answer.

And what about you, Harry, Harry Deiter? I need a
lung. I need a spleen, a couple of feet of intestine.
What would your answer be to your long lost
brother? Would you sign on the dotted line?

HARRY

What do you want me to say?

JASON

Evidently what I want is irrelevant. I'm just here
for spare parts, remember. What if you were the
one that was sick? Oh, I bet he'd be up here so
quick ... he'd pole-vault the border if he had to. All
for the sake of my kidney. Do you deny that?

HARRY

No. He loves me and would do anything for me.

JASON

He loves you like a son? And again, where do I fit
into this whole big picture? Replacement parts.
Face it, you never would have known about me, he
never would have revealed my existence if he
hadn't needed something from me. His cathartic

confession was one of convenience only. How do
you think that makes me feel?

HARRY

I'm sorry you feel that way.

JASON

You shouldn't be sorry for the truth. For your sake,
I hope he gets better. Your kids should have a
grandfather.

HARRY

He won't get better without your help.

JASON

I won't help.

HARRY

Stalemate.

JASON

Stalemate.

HARRY

Would money settle the stalemate? You were just
talking about thirty-one years of back child
support. I can get you some money. You can start
off your new life in style. How much do you want?

JASON

I don't believe you. You didn't hear a word I said, did you?

HARRY

Give me a week and I could get you ... what ... maybe forty thousand dollars. At least. And that's American! What would that be in Canadian, sixty thousand?

JASON

I don't want money.

HARRY

Give me some more time and ... and I might be able to get another twenty thousand, maybe some more. That's an awful lot of money to say no to.

JASON

No. Just ... just go. Leave me alone.

HARRY

At least consider it. Please.

JASON

Stop pleading with me. I don't know how many different ways to say it but I don't want any part of this. This is over ... just a waste of time.

JASON grabs HARRY's coat and tosses it to him.

I've got to finish packing.

HARRY is silent for a moment, just looking at his coat.

HARRY

What will I tell him?

JASON

The truth.

HARRY

The truth is going to kill him.

JASON

It kills all of us eventually. Maybe medical science will come through in the end. Maybe it won't be over.

HARRY

I thought you said I was the naive one.

JASON

Just trying to be positive.

HARRY

You're a coward.

JASON

If you want to think that, go ahead.

HARRY

All this time I've been thinking that maybe all you needed was a little convincing. That somewhere inside you … you would perceive the sheer humanity of why I'm here. And you're wrong about what I expected when I came up here. I didn't just expect you to jump up on a hospital bed and say "rip it out." I work in a hospital for Christ's sake. I see stuff like this every day.

JASON

But you're just a fund-raiser …

HARRY

You don't have to be in the boxing ring to get blood on you. I've done a lot of thinking about this. And you. And contrary to what you may believe, I do realize what I'm asking. But after all this arguing, in the end, it all comes down to you being a coward. You're afraid of him. Of me. Of what we represent. That's the truth, isn't it?

JASON

I thought you were leaving.

HARRY

My god, that's so simple. That's why all the hostility. You're resentful of me, because he picked me over you. That's it. And that hurts you. And that scares you even more.

JASON

Not me. I wasn't even part of the equation to begin with.

HARRY

At least be brave enough to admit your cowardice.

JASON

First of all, that's a contradiction in terms. Secondly, I'm tired of this.

HARRY

My father is a lot braver, lying there in a hospital bed, than you are.

JASON

There is no way that man is braver than me. He cheated on his wife, knocked up a woman, then ran away. And he denied it for over thirty years until it was convenient to remember. Till it would save his own neck. That does not sound like a brave man to me. They say guilt can make you sick. Maybe it's not his kidneys, maybe it's the guilt eating away at him. Maybe it's karma. Maybe it's God.

HARRY

I can hear the righteous indignation in your voice.
Your attempt at rationalization. You poor bastard.
You're still trying.

JASON

Don't confuse righteous indignation with
contempt.

HARRY

What I hear is a little boy who's bitter and angry at
the world and is trying to strike out at it in the
only way he can. By non-action. By not doing a
goddamned thing. Turning your back won't give
you peace of mind. You don't deserve to know my
father.

JASON

Are you quite done yet?

HARRY

You have a chance to do something noble, to be a
gracious human being. To put the wounded child
behind you.

JASON

I happen to like my wounded child. It's gotten me
through some tough times and it's been a better
friend to me than your father ever was. I'll keep my
wounded child and you keep your sick father. Go

back to America. Maybe you can invade another
third world country.

HARRY

I'll tell you something, Jason, I was hoping I'd like
you. Really I was. I'd never had a brother before.

JASON

You still don't. A brother is more than just a word.

HARRY

Maybe I am naive. Maybe my father did hurt you
with what he did. I can't deny that. But you've got
to heal sometime.

JASON

More fund-raising talk?

HARRY

No. Just the truth. Jason … Mr. Pierce, I don't like
you. Not because you refuse to help a dying old
man, but because I just don't think you're a nice
person. Simple as that. Maybe Bonnie figured that
out, too.

JASON

Okay, enough of this. Out. I want you out. Now.
Go.

*JASON starts pushing HARRY hard towards
the door, almost knocking him off his feet. He
opens the door and pushes HARRY out into the
hallway.*

Goodbye, Harry, Harry Deiter. You've worn out
your welcome, I'm afraid. As my mother would say,
it's been swell but the swelling's gone down.

HARRY

Are you going to tell your mother about this?

JASON

No.

HARRY

Why not?

JASON

It didn't happen.

HARRY

But it did.

JASON

Maybe in your world, but not in mine. I've already
forgotten you, and your father.

HARRY

Your father, too.

JASON

> My father was my grandfather. That was more than enough for me. And for the record, I don't think there are any unknown grandkids running around this country. He had integrity. I think your father is the coward for telling you only now. And not telling your mother. She has a right to know. Now get the fuck out before I call Immigration.

HARRY

> I wish …

> > *JASON slams the door shut violently. HARRY is gone.*
> > *JASON pauses a moment before finding a chair to sit. He is emotionally shaken and tries to gather his strength. It's a few seconds before he tries to finish packing again. He disappears into the bedroom. While he's gone, somewhere in the apartment, HARRY's phone starts to ring. JASON pops back into the room, puzzled, then remembers that HARRY's phone was tossed into a pile of boxes during the earlier fight. He rummages through the boxes and finally finds it, still ringing. He holds it for a few seconds in his hand, wondering what to do. Hesitantly, he answers the phone.*

JASON

> Hello?

JASON is uncomfortable, not really knowing why he's doing this.

No ma'am, my name is uh … Jason. (*Pause.*) Uh … your son's not here right now. He must have forgotten his phone here. (*Pause.*) No, I don't think he's taking the train. It would be an awfully long train ride. (*Pause.*) Me? Just a friend, I guess. (*Pause.*) How do I know him … That's a long story. Are you sure you really want to know? Ma'am, perhaps you'd better sit down for this one.

JASON sits himself down on a chair, ready for a long conversation.

End of Act One.

ACT TWO

*Lights up on the same apartment. Maybe with
a few more packed boxes. JASON is piling
boxes near the door. He takes a drink from a
beer. Beside the beer is a pizza carton.
Suddenly there is a vicious pounding at the
door. JASON smiles and takes a comfortable seat
at the other end of the room, nursing his beer
and grabbing a slice of pizza. The loud
knocking continues at the doorway.*

JASON

It's open.

*A very angry and distraught HARRY enters,
practically livid.*

HARRY

You bastard!

JASON

Technically, that's correct. Problems, Harry, Harry
Deiter?

HARRY

You told her! You told my mother everything.

JASON

    Was that a problem?

HARRY

    My god, you don't know what you've done. Why?!

JASON

    A family should have no secrets. You look like you
    could use a beer.

HARRY

    My mother collapsed. She's under a doctor's care
    now.

JASON

    That was not my intention. Honestly. She did take
    it kind of hard. The truth can be uncomfortable.
    But if you're gonna collapse, I guess the hospital's
    the place to do it.

HARRY

    You had no right to do that. My god ...

JASON

    I believe this is your phone. And I hope you don't
    mind, I used it to order a pizza. I was kind of
    hungry and well, my phone is dead. Uncooked
    Kraft noodles don't quite do the trick. There's still a
    slice left if you're interested.

JASON tosses him the phone.

HARRY

> This is a nightmare. Everything … a nightmare.
> What did my mother ever do to you?

JASON

> Oh, don't be so melodramatic. You're making it
> sound like a conspiracy. Oh, I'd better warn you,
> this is Canadian beer. Better watch yourself. It
> contains alcohol.

HARRY

> You called my mother on my own phone … just
> to be cruel? I don't understand why you …

JASON

> Actually, she phoned me … or you, technically. You
> should be careful where you leave your phone. Bad
> things could happen. She seemed like a very nice
> woman. I think she and my mother would have
> gotten along wonderfully. Ironic, isn't it?

HARRY

> I should kick the living shit out of you.

JASON

> How American, but that wouldn't help their
> situation very much, now would it? Or yours
> either. Sure you don't want that beer?

HARRY

You smug son of a bitch …

JASON

That kind of language will get you nowhere. You've told me how your mother is, how's your father?

HARRY is too angry to respond.

Not much of a change, huh? Well, I've got my fingers crossed for the both of you. Really I do. These are rough times for your family. I sympathize.

HARRY grabs JASON and pushes him up against a wall, with every intention of doing some great physical harm.

HARRY

This is unacceptable. You are dangerous.

JASON

Careful. You might hurt my kidneys.

HARRY

You had no right to tell my mother. No right!

JASON pushes him away.

JASON

> I had every right. So now she's been dragged kicking and screaming into this mess like I have. Being lied to by her husband and son. She has every right to know. I just had the guts you and your father didn't. You, on the other hand, had no right to invade my life with your fucking soap opera and issue me ultimatums.

HARRY

> I never gave you any ultimatums!!

JASON

> What do you think "You've got to help him or he'll die" sounds like? Evidently sometime when I wasn't looking I suddenly became responsible for the life and death of somebody I've never met. I'm a cook in Canada … that's all. He is not my responsibility. And it's not me your father should be seeking absolution from, it's your mother. Me and my mom got over him a long time ago.

HARRY

> But my mother … She …

JASON

> … deserved to know. Even you should be able to figure that out. You said it happened a long time ago and he's a different man now, then she should

be able to figure all this out and forgive him.
Besides, you don't think she wouldn't have noticed?

HARRY

Noticed what?

JASON

Noticed that her hubby is home. Surprisingly well
and fit. With a large, unusual scar where his kidney
was. You were married once. Don't wives tend to
notice those things? You don't think it would occur
to her to inquire what the hell happened? Face it,
Harry, she would have figured it out eventually. I
just ripped the Band-Aid off quickly, where you
would have made it more painful in the end. And I
didn't know your nickname was Squeam.

HARRY

What ... what are you talking about?

JASON

You were always squeamish about baiting a hook
with a live worm, so your father called you
Squeam. Kind of a cute story. You're from New
England, man, I thought you guys eat, drink and
shit fish.

HARRY

You don't use worms for that kind of fishing. And
not everybody from New England is involved in

the fishing industry. And my mother told you about
my nickname ... ?

JASON

Yep, I didn't drop the bomb on her immediately.
That would've been cruel. We chit-chatted a bit.
We even talked about bread making. Like I said
earlier, I wanted to know a bit more about you ...
and him. How's your prostate?

HARRY

That was a false alarm.

JASON

Still, you can't be too careful. Squeamish subject.
And actually, the reason your mother called in the
first place was to remind you to pick up some of
those pastries she likes at her favourite bakery ...
here in New York. She was disappointed in more
ways than one when I told her you weren't in New
York. But there are several good, if not excellent,
bakeries here in Toronto. She didn't seem overly
impressed.

HARRY

My god ... you're enjoying this. Why are you
enjoying this?

*JASON gets up and goes to his refrigerator. He
gets out two beers and tosses one to HARRY.*

JASON

> I don't know. I always thought I was a nice guy.
> Contrary to what some of my exes might say.
> But then again, my life was rather uncomplicated
> until you showed up. And here we are. So I guess
> technically, we could say you started the ball
> rolling. By boarding that plane to Toronto. Or your
> father started it by confessing it to you on his sick
> bed. Or I started it by being born. Or your father
> started it by flying up to Canada and meeting my
> mom. Or …

HARRY

> Stop it! This is not a joke. It's not.

JASON

> I think it is a joke, a hilarious joke, and we're just
> waiting for the punch line.

HARRY

> This is going to devastate my mother. Why did you
> have to bring her into this, you sick bastard?

JASON

> She was already neck deep in this. She was in this
> long before I was born. When she phoned, and the
> more I talked to her, I couldn't help picturing my
> mother in her position. And I figured, well, to
> quote an old Native therapy saying, "before the

healing can take place, the poison must be exposed." So I exposed the poison. I was doing her a favour, though unfortunately the process can be a little painful. Like going to the dentist.

HARRY

The doctor had to sedate her. That's doing her a favour?! So you rationalize doing this horrible thing to my mother because of some fucking Indian philosophy. That's sick. You're sick. This whole situation is sick.

JASON

I'm not sure I understand it myself, but it seemed like the right decision at the time. Look at it this way, given the choice, do you wish your precious father had decided to take the knowledge of me to his grave? Would you be better off not knowing about me and your father's indiscretions?

HARRY

I ... I ... can't answer that.

JASON

It's not that difficult a question. I could easily carry on with my life not knowing his name was Lawrence Deiter. No skin off my nose. But that's just me. And your mother certainly could have lived without the news. But maybe you're right.

Maybe I'm just not a very nice person after all …
but think about how shocking that realization is to
me. To see your true nature. What you're capable
of. Hey, your beer's getting warm.

HARRY ignores the beer.

It might help calm you down.

HARRY

I'm not thirsty.

JASON

What does thirsty have to do with drinking beer?

HARRY

This is … this is … un-fucking-believable.

JASON

You're just realizing this?

HARRY

I phoned the hospital once I got to the airport.
From a pay phone. To check on my father. He
sounded funny on the phone, different. He
sounded old, very old. And weak. I think my
mother was giving him the strength to fight, they
had been through so much together. And now that
she knows, and he knows she knows, he might not
be able to fight this battle without her. You don't

know what you've set in motion. He said she just
stood there beside his bed, tears in her eyes,
muttering over and over again, "Thirty-seven years.
Thirty-seven years." Then she passed out. Is this
what you wanted? Is this the justice you were
seeking?

JASON

No. It's just an unfortunate side effect. Collateral
damage, as they say.

HARRY

Then why did you tell her? I told you why we
didn't. In fact you went out of your way to tell her,
and this is exactly what we thought would happen.
And don't give me any crap about it was for her
own good. This does not do a sixty-year-old
woman good.

JASON

My mother is diabetic, lactose intolerant and a
recovering alcoholic. She smokes, and watches way
too much television for her own health. She's had
her gall bladder removed. So I know a few things
about a sick mother. And I've heard some of my
uncles say her drinking problem started with your
father and his unique approach to child rearing. If
I'm to blame for your mother's breakdown, then I
accept that. A reaction follows an action, I guess.

But I was trying to do something constructive. And
for the sake of argument, let's say you're right, that I
told her to get even, then that too is a reaction to
an action. What's your father's excuse?

HARRY

For the sake of argument … hell! You were just
trying to hurt him … me … through her.

JASON

I was not.

HARRY

I think you actually believe that. You do, don't you?

JASON

Drink your beer.

HARRY

Fuck the beer. You have ruined my family. Are you
proud?

JASON

Again you're exaggerating. There's another old
Native saying I've heard elders use when good or
bad things happen: "It was meant to be." I've never
really understood that one because it kind of takes
away the importance of free will. I mean if it was
meant to be, then why bother doing anything, if

"it," whatever "it" is, was meant to be. It will just
"be," without any help from us. So what's the
point? Oh, but what do I know? Maybe this was all
meant to be? Do you get where I'm coming from,
Squeam? Is this too much Indian 101?

HARRY

So breaking my mother's heart was meant to be?
So by that reasoning, my being here, in your
apartment, soliciting help for my father was meant
to be. It must be or otherwise, if I'd been a couple
of hours late, I might have missed you entirely. So,
according to your philosophy, you were meant to
help my father.

JASON

Hold on there, Kemosabe. The "It was meant to
be" philosophy only works for Native people.
Manifest Destiny is your bag.

HARRY

How convenient for you. You seem to be absolved
from all responsibility.

JASON

It comes with being an oppressed minority. You
should try it sometime, Harry, Harry Deiter ...
Deiter, what is that ... German? And here I am
talking to you about oppressed minorities.

HARRY

Don't give me that. My father's family were on this
continent way before either World War.

JASON

Congratulations. So were my mother's.

HARRY

Don't forget, you're half-German, too.

JASON

Biologically. Every other cell. So that means I'm
only German on even-numbered days.

HARRY

That half-white part of you, doesn't that give
you some responsibility? Or are these genes
conveniently overshadowed by your Indian genes?
The one good apple makes the whole barrel
edible?

JASON

Ya. Das is goot. I like that. I may use it sometime.
Except you shouldn't use the term "apple" when
you're talking about Native people.

HARRY

So you have taken no account of your Caucasian
half?

JASON

That's not who I am.

HARRY

You must be joking. When my father first told me about you, about you being Indian, I had images of …

JASON

Me on a horse with a case of beer, killing buffalo?

HARRY

I'm not that stupid. I've read Sherman Alexie. But when you opened that door … you definitely were not what I was expecting. Your white heritage is quite apparent, t-shirts excepted.

JASON

Through no fault of my own. I was raised on a reserve by an Ojibway family. That is who I am. Never judge a book by its cover.

HARRY

Clichés won't help you. And you've never wondered about your white half? The half that's lying in a hospital bed a thousand miles away?

JASON

Not for a moment. I knew who I was. How many people can actually say that? Can you?

HARRY

> This bantering is ridiculous. My father's going to die ... my mother is ... I don't know how my mother is ... all because of you. This was a terrible mistake. I can't believe my father's fate is in your hands. You're one fucked-up guy.

JASON

> And you've only been here a couple of hours. Give it time.
>
> *At this point, HARRY's cell phone rings.*
>
> Cell phones ... aren't they amazing things? You'd better answer it. Could be important.
>
> *HARRY answers his phone.*

HARRY

> Hello ... oh, hi Arlene. I'm ... (*Pause.*) Oh Christ, already ... I forgot ... I can't really ... (*Pause.*) My father. But ... Yes, yes, I know. Put him on.
>
> *Feeling a little uncomfortable, HARRY wanders to the far side of the room to complete his call.*
>
> Hey soldier ... how's my little man? (*Pause.*) Yes, I know it's Friday night but Daddy's away right now. (*Pause.*) No, farther away. Up north. In Canada. (*Pause.*) No, there's no snow. It's September, Colin. I know tonight's my night to tell you a story but

Daddy's kind of busy right now. What say we do this tomorrow, huh, Soldier? (*Pause.*) I know but I'll make it a really good one tomorrow. I promise. What do you want to be tomorrow? (*Pause.*) A cowboy ... okay, tomorrow night, I'll tell you a story about cowboys. I promise. Now give Daddy a goodbye kiss now. (*Pause.*) Daddy loves you too, Colin. Bye.

HARRY hangs up the phone.

JASON

Your son?

HARRY

Yeah.

JASON

He likes cowboys?

HARRY

Sometimes. He's got a great imagination. Every Friday night I tell him a story. Either in person or over the phone. Since Arlene and I separated, he's been feeling a little insecure about not seeing me as much as he wants to. So I tell him these stories about the two of us running off and joining the circus or something like that. Last week we were going to become astronauts.

JASON

> And tomorrow you're going to be cowboys. Ask him if he's ever wanted to run off and become an Indian. He's got an uncle that can teach him.

HARRY

> Maybe if you had kids, you'd understand the bond between a father and a son.

JASON

> Hmm, do you think maybe if I had a father I'd understand the bond between a father and a son?

> > *HARRY is silent.*

> (*delighted*) Two points, Jason. So now what? You've got your phone. Are we done with our little tête-à-tête? Wow, that's two in less than a couple of hours. What does that average out to? About fifteen years a visit?

HARRY

> It's a cruel world, Jason. I didn't realize it rested on your shoulders.

JASON

> I'm an illegitimate half-breed Indian that grew up on a dirt-water reserve in the middle of nowhere with a single alcoholic parent. You get used to it. When does the next plane to Providence leave?

HARRY

> 8:30.

JASON

> With traffic and customs, sure you're gonna make it? Better leave now if I were you.

>> *Again HARRY is silent. Then he takes the phone and starts dialling.*

> Calling a cab?

HARRY

> Not quite. (*Pause.*) Hello Dad. You okay? (*Pause.*) How's Mom? (*Pause.*) Tell her I'll be there as soon as I can. I'm here right now. Sorry it took so long but the traffic in this town is horrible. Hold on.

>> *HARRY holds out the phone to the startled JASON, who backs away.*

JASON

> What ... no ...

HARRY

> Take it. He's flesh and blood. If nothing else, maybe it'll give you closure.

>> *JASON continues to avoid the phone like it has the plague.*

What's the matter? Maybe this call was meant to be. Afraid of him?

HARRY holds the phone right in front of JASON. JASON hesitates for a second, then slowly grabs the phone. A second passes before he brings it up to his mouth.

HARRY

What are you going to say?

JASON

I don't know you.

He then turns off the phone and hands it back to HARRY.

That was easier than I thought. Sounds like closure to me.

HARRY

I just hope, ten years from now, when maybe you have your own children … you don't regret what you've just done. Because he won't be around for a second chance.

JASON

Regret. Now there's an interesting word. Do you want to know what the definition of regret is? When I lived in Ottawa, I had a good friend. His name was Scott. Scott Small Pike from Manitoba.

We worked together at a Native catering company.
Poor Scott was adopted. And after a few years, he
decided to seek out his biological parents. He was
nervous but he managed to do the paperwork and
ask the right questions. So one day, a day very
similar to today, a middle-aged man answered a
knock at his door, kinda like I did. Standing there
was Scott, this man's son. Scott nervously
introduced himself to the man and waited for a
reaction. He got one. The man didn't care.
Evidently there was a reason Scott had been put up
for adoption, he wasn't wanted. And it seemed little
had changed over twenty-six years. The man closed
the door after less than five minutes. And Scott
went home to his apartment like he did every
night, only this time it seemed a little more empty.
He said he always regretted the decision to find his
parents. Said he was better off not knowing.

HARRY

I disagree with your friend. In many ways I think
it's better to know and be disappointed than not
know and wonder. That could drive you insane.

JASON

You're not Scott. And you're not me. Last I heard,
Scott had given up on trying to find his mother.
Why have your heart broken twice when once is
sufficient?

HARRY

That's a different situation.

JASON

You're right. Somehow I don't think Scott's father would have the nerve to ask for a kidney. I don't believe he'd think he deserved one. But then again, it's all relative, isn't it? Oh look, I made a joke.

JASON checks his watch.

Oh geez, is it that time already?! The truck is due here in an hour and I've still got a bunch to do. Bonnie had offered to help me pack but I think that would have been a little uncomfortable. That's my Bonnie, she can rationalize breaking your heart one minute but can still be nice till the end. I'm still finding odds and ends of her stuff scattered about. I'm sort of weeding her existence out of my apartment and my life. These are the slippers I gave her last Christmas. My mother made them. I wonder why she didn't take them. She must have forgotten.

JASON tosses the slippers into a box marked "Bonnie's Stuff." He grabs an empty box and goes into the kitchen and starts emptying drawers.

JASON

I've gotta finish all this before the truck arrives.

HARRY

Your Bonnie. Was she First Nations or white?

JASON

What possible difference could that make?

HARRY

I think it would say volumes about you,
psychologically speaking. They say "you are who
you date." I'll believe this Indian thing of yours if
she's Native … but if she's not … if she's Caucasian
… that's a whole different kettle of fish. An
interesting kettle of fish. Arlene was white, first
generation Dutch to be specific. I admit it freely.
So tell me, truthfully, what was Bonnie?

JASON

Korean.

*JASON reaches into one of the packing boxes
and brings out a picture.*

Kimchee and wild rice. You should try it sometime.
You don't believe me, that's her. Christ, she looked
more Indian than I did. So where does that fit into
your amateur psychoanalysis?

HARRY

I don't know.

JASON

Give it up, Harry, Harry Deiter. It's been a long day for both of us. Have you got anything more to add to the discussion?

HARRY

I guess I've said everything I came here to say. And you've said everything you've had to say. And nothing's changed.

JASON

Will I ever see you again, Harry, Harry Deiter? Or is the issue of a needed kidney the only reason you would ever come and visit?

HARRY

I hope I never see you again.

JASON

I never wanted to see you in the first place. Don't forget your phone. Have fun building your hospitals.

HARRY puts his phone in his coat pocket.

HARRY

> You realize if I walk out that door, alone, you've all but killed your own father.

JASON

> Silly man. How can I kill somebody who never existed?

HARRY

> He exists. He's real. He's alive. He's my father. He's a grandfather. He's a loving husband. Why can't you see that? He deserves to live, damn you!

JASON

> Everybody deserves to live. But he doesn't deserve my kidney. I'd give one ... or both to my mother before the doctor's words finished echoing from the walls. I wouldn't have to consciously even think about it. But not to him. He hasn't earned them. But if you want, I'll think of him every time I pee.

HARRY

> Is that what this is all about? He hasn't earned them. Are you penalizing him because he's your father?

JASON

> He's not my father. My grandfather was my father.

HARRY

What if he were a stranger?

JASON

What are you talking about?

HARRY

Oh come on, Jason. If somebody came to you, saying you and only you had the chance to save a human life. Let's say he's a complete stranger. And it would only involve two or three weeks of discomfort, but a man would be alive because of you, you would have saved a life. Would you do it then? For somebody you didn't know?

JASON turns away and rearranges some boxes.

Sitting around the waiting room at the hospital, thinking of our options, we've talked about possibilities like this. And I don't know what this says about the difference between me and you, but if I could, I'd make the choice to save a life.

JASON

Because you build hospitals.

HARRY

But you ...

JASON

> But nothing. I'm not here to discuss medical ethics.
> That situation is not this situation. You love this
> man, and you think I hate him. I don't. The
> opposite of love is not hate, it's indifference. And
> I'm very indifferent. What I would do in another
> situation ... ask me again when that situation
> comes up. You're beginning to annoy me now and
> I'm not even close to finishing all this packing.

HARRY

> You won't do it of your own free will. You don't
> want money. You won't listen to logic. What will it
> take to help my family? Just tell me.

> *Pause.*

JASON

> This is Bonnie's corkscrew. Now she'd give you a
> kidney. You know, I think it hurts twice as bad
> when somebody who's really nice leaves you and
> breaks your heart than when it's a severely nasty
> break-up. Why is that, do you think? Maybe
> because you're free to hate them or something. I
> just wish she'd been a secret porn star or drug
> trafficker or something concrete to dislike. It's hard
> to resent somebody that left you a tray of freshly
> baked muffins when she moved out. Low-fat ones,
> too. That reminds me, this is her muffin tray.

He puts the tray and corkscrew in Bonnie's box.
He looks in the cupboard.

Oh god, I've still got some cat food. She got
custody of Stubbs. Reserves aren't good for cats.
Too many dogs. What the hell am I going to do
with this stuff ... do you want some cat food? You
strike me as a cat kind of guy.

HARRY

No. I've got two beagles.

JASON

Do you think your dog would notice it was cat
food? Or vice versa? I'd hate for this to go to
waste. What do you do with leftover cat food, I
wonder? A food bank? Would they take it? Is there
a food bank for pets, I wonder? I know. I'll leave it
in the lobby with a sign saying it's up for grabs.

HARRY

I don't care about your stupid cat food. My father
is essentially dead. There are no other options left.

JASON

You're mourning a bit early, Harry, Harry Deiter.
Like I said, medicine's a fabulous thing. Hope for
the best.

HARRY

He did ask me for something, when I met you. Regardless of the outcome of our meeting.

JASON

Yeah.

HARRY

He wants a picture.

JASON

Of what?

HARRY

Of you.

JASON

He wants a picture of me?! Why?

HARRY

He wanted to see your face … what you looked like. I guess to see what might have been. He did ask. So, do you have one I can have?

JASON

A picture. He wants a picture of me?

HARRY

> You won't look at a picture of him, but he's more
> than interested in having one of you. Well? It's
> getting late.

> *JASON hesitates, unsure of what to do. Finally,*
> *he moves a few boxes around, till he selects the*
> *appropriate one. He opens it and fishes around*
> *in it until he pulls out an envelope, thick with*
> *pictures. He selects one and offers it to HARRY.*

JASON

> Fine. He wants a picture of me. He can have one. I
> don't care, I've got doubles. Here. This one was
> taken last summer down by the lake on my reserve.
> He's probably been there. Tell him to enjoy.

> *JASON returns to packing. HARRY studies the*
> *picture for a second.*

HARRY

> Hmm, you look like a darker version of my father,
> when he was younger.

JASON

> Don't say that.

HARRY

> It's true.

JASON

I don't want it to be true.

HARRY

My hair was always lighter. Evidence of my
mother's Scandinavian background, I guess.

JASON

Ummm ... Is he ... is he bald?

HARRY

Who?

JASON

You know who. Him.

HARRY

Dad? Like a billiard ball.

JASON

Oh fuck! That's not good for an Aboriginal. Bad
kidneys and baldness ... thanks for the legacy, Dad.
I got that on one side, and my mother's diabetes
and lactose intolerance on the other. Man, I'm
playing against a stacked deck.

HARRY

Well, you can relax. Baldness is passed down
through the female gene. Trust me, I've done the

research. You will probably get to keep your
precious First Nations hair.

JASON

Well, you've got your picture. Anything else?

HARRY

Just one more thing. He said to say he's sorry.

JASON

He's sorry?!

JASON starts to laugh loudly.

He's sorry?! For what—my life?! Well, good for
him. Excellent. Tell him I'm sorry, too. But it's too
late for being sorry. He's dying and I'm beyond
caring that he's sorry. But if it makes him feel good
to be sorry ... all the more power to him. (*Pause.*)
How dare he be "sorry"?! He should be more than
sorry. He should be fucking miserably depressed
and sitting on the ledge of his hospital room
window ready to jump. He can keep his sorry. I
don't want it. If you're not going to drink that
fucking beer, I will.

*JASON grabs the beer and opens it viciously
and drinks.*

HARRY

He is sorry.

JASON

Shut up. Just shut up.

HARRY

Jason?

JASON

No!

HARRY

I'm sorry, too. For what he did. And I'm sorry for
what it's done to you. I can't make amends for
what happened thirty years ago, and neither can he.
You're letting it eat away at you.

JASON

What are you talking about? Nothing's eating away
at me. I was perfectly fine until you arrived. You'll
notice it's been downhill in my life ever since you
knocked on my door. Once you leave, things will
be fine again. You can believe that.

HARRY

No. You don't work in a hospital for nine years
without picking up a few things about how the
mind works. You're angry. Very angry.

JASON

Of course I'm angry. A stranger wants my kidney.
That would make anybody angry. Quit trying to

psychoanalyze me. You're barking up the wrong
tree, my friend.

HARRY

No, it's more than that. You're ... what ... thirty-
one. Not married. No kids. Living from one
apartment to the next. Same with a job ...
girlfriends ... cities ... Moving from one life to
another. When something pisses you off, you move.
You don't seem to want to put down any roots.

JASON

I've got roots. I'm moving back to them in a few
minutes. That'll do me just fine.

HARRY

Yet I live within a half-hour of where I grew up.
Career, family. It's all there for me. It seems I'm the
opposite of you.

JASON

Your father's dying. You've had a bad divorce. Your
kids live with your ex-wife. And one kid might be
scarred by the divorce ... Yeah, I envy you. There's
just so much there I want ... You're reaching,
Squeam.

HARRY

No, it's not that much of a reach. You're just not
much of a commitment guy, are you? When

Bonnie said she wanted closure with that other guy
… did you ask her to stay?

JASON

Why? She'd made her decision. I wasn't going to
beg.

HARRY

Oh Jason, some people just want to be comforted,
want some reassurance. If you had kids, you'd
understand that. They want confirmation, security.
Maybe the closure Bonnie was looking for wasn't
with the park ranger. Maybe it was with you.
Maybe she didn't forget the slippers. Maybe she left
them behind on purpose. So you could bring them
to her.

JASON

You've known me for all of an hour and already
you're telling me how to live my life. I think your
life needs more repair than mine, Squeam.

HARRY

Hey, even getting a divorce takes a certain amount
of commitment. My father, my kids, my job. My
whole life is commitment.

JASON

I commit. I'm very committed.

HARRY

To what?

JASON

I have a mother. A career. Being a cook is a career.
When I have a girlfriend, I'm committed to her ...

HARRY

Except for the occasional trip to a hockey
tournament.

JASON

I told you, that happened once. Once. Anyways,
I'm just as committed as you are to your life. It's
just another kind of commitment. So I don't have a
bunch of RRSPs or a new car. Big deal. I'm saving
up to get life insurance, but these things take time.
But tell the truth, how happy are you with your
precious committed life?

HARRY

Other than my father's health, and the failure of my
marriage, it's the life I made. I'm content.

JASON

There's a non-committal term if I've ever heard
one. "I'm content." The world's full of content
people, and few happy ones. I would think being
content is the equivalent of mowing the grass in
your slogan. How can you condone that then?

HARRY

> Nine-tenths of the world aren't content. It's the difference between being a child and being a man. A child is only concerned with looking after themselves. "To be happy, I want what I want right now." A man has responsibilities. Those responsibilities may take away from his own immediate happiness, but in the end, there's a much better payoff. For instance, paying a mortgage rather than rent. Taking your daughter to skating lessons at 8:00 on a Sunday morning even though you were at a cocktail party till 2:00 the night before. So I'm not living the hedonistic lifestyle of a rock star, but in the end, when I go to bed, I know I've made the world a better place, both personally and professionally. Can you say that? I build hospitals. Indirectly, I save lives. I've made a difference.

JASON

> So, you're a glorified panhandler. I give money to people I see begging on the street. I help them eat that night. Indirectly, I save lives too.

> *JASON lifts up a bag of clothes.*

> See this? This is going to Goodwill. I help this world in my own way. Recycling.

*He kicks a box, and the rattling of bottles can
be heard.*

Grass roots stuff like that. I just don't do it in a suit.
You can keep your American hospitals because,
from what I hear, only the rich can afford to use a
hospital down there. But everybody up here that I
know can always use a good sweatshirt and some
change for coffee.

HARRY

Okay, so you're a big-time philanthropist. The great
donator of First Nations–themed t-shirts and Tim
Hutton's coffee …

JASON

It's Horton! Tim Hortons!!!

HARRY

Tim Hortons then. But what really … (*Pause.*) Tim
Horton? Wasn't he a hockey player? Back in the
'60s? The Maple Leafs, right?

JASON

You know that? How do you know that? Most
Canadians don't remember that.

HARRY

My father is a big hockey fan. He used to go to all
the games in Boston. I think he saw the Leafs play

against the Bruins a couple of times. And now
Horton's selling coffee … wow … well, it worked
for Joe Dimaggio, I guess.

JASON

That's the guy who was married to Marilyn
Monroe.

HARRY

I think you're thinking of Arthur Miller, the writer.

JASON

Really, I didn't know he was married to her. Bonnie
was reading one of his books a while ago, I think it
was a travel book. The Tropic of something.

HARRY

No, that's … Henry Miller.

JASON

Henry Miller was married to Marilyn Monroe?

HARRY

No, he … what?

*JASON rummages around in his trash basket,
finally locating a used Tim Hortons travel coffee
cup. He shows it to HARRY.*

JASON

> It doesn't matter. The great Tim Horton's been
> dead for thirty years. It's a long story. But coffee
> and hockey. Welcome to Canada. Two of the few
> obsessions common to both Native and non-Native
> Canadians. Where do you think iced coffee came
> from?

HARRY

> I don't care. I'm wasting my time here. I don't
> think I have anything left to say.

JASON

> If he doesn't have this operation, how long does he
> have to live?

HARRY

> It's hard to say. A couple of months at best. Maybe
> a little longer. Maybe not.

JASON

> So he likes hockey?

HARRY

> Very much.

JASON

> Well, I guess he can't be all that bad then.

HARRY

Very Canadian of you.

JASON

I've never actually seen a professional game in person. Seen a million amateur games, played in a couple of dozen myself. But never got around to seeing an actual professional game. That's also on my list of things to do.

HARRY

I've been to a few.

JASON

Lucky you.

HARRY

Yeah, lucky me. Look …

JASON

Harry?

HARRY

Yes.

JASON

If I've been a little stressed out today, sorry. I read an article once on how moving day is one of, if not the most, stressful days a person can endure. Worse than the day of your marriage, even of a funeral.

HARRY

Yeah, I've heard that too.

JASON

Your arrival has not helped the situation much.

HARRY

I guess not. I can see the shock. My last couple of months haven't exactly been stress-free. My father, coming up here, the two hours I spent on the plane, the taxi ride over here thinking about this. There were a thousand other things I would rather be doing and a thousand other places I would rather have been. But I had a responsibility. I had to do this.

JASON

Again with responsibilities. I would have done the same for my mother, I suppose. It's hard to say right now. I think I'm numb. The news, the arguing, the phone calls, I don't feel anything at the moment. It's been quite the day. Harry?

HARRY

Yeah?

JASON

Do you really dislike me?

HARRY

You've made it very hard to like you.

JASON

Maybe it's just the circumstances. You must admit, these aren't quite normal circumstances. Maybe if we met at a hockey game or something …

HARRY

Possible but unlikely. Stress can bring out the best in a person or the worst. It shows what a person is really like, underneath everything.

JASON

What are you going to tell your father about me? Other than the fact you're not that impressed with me.

HARRY

That you're angry. That you're alone. That you don't want to know him. That you don't care. That you like hockey. Have I left anything out?

JASON

No. That just about covers everything, I guess. Tell him, I guess, you reap what you sow.

HARRY

I hope you remember that, too.

JASON

And tell him …

HARRY

Yes …

JASON

… never mind.

HARRY

Any words for my mother?

JASON

Ah yes, your mother. No. I think I've said enough
to her. Maybe I do have some anger issues. I wish
her well. Honest, I do.

HARRY

Perhaps getting some therapy should be on your
to-do list.

JASON

Nah, I'm okay. Things will be great once I get
home. I'm a survivor.

They study each other for a moment.

You know, from this angle, you sort of do look like me. Taller, paler, better-dressed, but it's there.

HARRY

Only three years' difference. Well, I have to go see a sick man. Can't miss this flight. The next plane doesn't leave until tomorrow morning.

HARRY puts on his coat and gets ready to leave.

JASON

Goodbye Harry, Harry Deiter. Squeam. Squeam sounds like an Indian name.

HARRY stops at the door.

HARRY

Before I go, one last time. After everything that's happened tonight ... I have to ask. Won't you please reconsider? You are his last chance. Take the test.

JASON

What if I did? And what if I was perfect for this transplant thing? What then?

HARRY

Possibly an operation.

JASON

> I mean after that. There we'd be, lying in matching hospital beds, a few feet from each other. There'd be your mother there, too, looking at me, a symbol of your father's betrayal. And part of that betrayal stitched to his body. She'd think of me and my mother every time she saw the scar. Do you think she'd be happy with that? For the rest of her days?

HARRY

> She'd be happy he was alive. That's all that's important right now.

JASON

> I don't know, Squeam. Would your father take me out to a hockey game? Take me fishing like he took you? You see, I entered this picture a little too late. And under a dark and desperate cloud. Good things do not come from dark and desperate clouds. I'd be out a kidney, and you'd have a brother your family didn't want. Not the best of situations.

HARRY

> We'd make it work. Yes, it would be awkward, I admit that. But considering the alternative ...

JASON

> Yes, considering the alternative .... I think that's what you should do, my friend. Consider

alternatives. Let me see that picture. The one of
him in your wallet.

*Eagerly, HARRY takes his wallet out and shows
a picture to JASON. JASON takes the picture
and looks at it a good long time. HARRY is
hopeful.*

JASON

My god, he really is bald.

HARRY

He's your father.

JASON looks at it a long time again.

JASON

He's not what I thought he'd look like.

HARRY

He's lost a lot of weight since that picture was
taken. This time next month ... he might be dead.

JASON

... dead.

HARRY

One little blood test ... Jason. If you don't do this,
everything you've said to me today, about him,
about yourself and your mother ... you might regret
it someday. If he dies, and you haven't done anything

to help him, you will have to live with that for the rest of your life. By running away, aren't you committing the same sin you accuse my father of?

JASON

I guess I am ...

JASON closes the wallet and hands it back to HARRY.

But let me tell you a story. When I was a kid, there was this old man that lived near my mother's house on the reserve. There was nothing really special about him, just an old man living by himself in a house ... a very old house. So old that the house didn't have any running water or plumbing. Got all his water from a well a little ways from his house. The village had always offered to install plumbing but he didn't want it. He didn't trust the things they put in the water, this was about the time they were introducing fluoride and all that stuff in our community. "Ground water tastes better too," he'd say. Just an old man and his well. The sad thing is, me and my cousins, whenever he was away at the store or sleeping, would pee in his well. There was no point to it but we did it anyways. We weren't bad kids, just bored. And he wasn't a bad man, just a loner. It was just something to do on hot summer days. I guess I do poison wells. Goodbye, Squeam.

HARRY

Goodbye Jason. I hope you can live with yourself.

JASON

Well, Harry, I have so far.

> *He closes the door on HARRY. Then he pauses, gathering his strength, and starts stacking boxes. He hits the stereo "on" button and music is heard throughout the apartment.*
>
> *A few seconds pass before JASON can't continue with the boxes. Trying something different, he cranks up the music, trying to block his thoughts. He grabs one of his immaculately packed garbage bags, but it isn't long before frustration, anger and a few other emotions he can't name overcome him. He suddenly rips open the bag of clothes, sending the neatly folded t-shirts and other clothes flying across the room. He ends up sliding down into a nearby chair, wracked with emotion. He doesn't know what he feels, as many conflicting feelings take control. Wave after wave washes over him until he dissolves into an emotional mess and collapses into tears.*
>
> *Lights go down.*

THE END.